/=|O⁀⁀° **You can draw**
lines, circles, curves, so...

You can

CRESSRELLES PUBLISHING COMPANY LIMITED
Kestrels House, Stoke Row Road, Peppard Common, Henley-on-Thames, Oxfordshire
© 1973 Brian Paine, Leslie Smith
ISBN 0·85956·001·5
Printed by Burgess & Son (Abingdon) Ltd

abcg236ZS

You can write letters and numbers, so...

draw the seaside

This book will show how easy it is

Look at the letters and numbers which you use everyday. See how they are all made up from straight lines and curves. Practise drawing them. It can be fun doing just that and you can make so many shapes and patterns.

Make your drawings as large as you like. Use big sheets of paper and felt pens, coloured pencils, paints or anything else.

Now let's make something with only straight lines

fit them together to make a boat like this. Each new line will be in colour.

That's easy - now practise drawing some more. Make some of them different.

Now let's draw a simple curve

and some more curves.

If we join them together we shall have some water.

A boat and some water – we could be at the seaside. Let's draw a sandcastle, we only need some more straight lines.

To build a sandcastle we must have a bucket and spade. We have almost drawn the bucket already. We use straight lines and a curve for these but they are very easy, aren't they! Fill them in with coloured scribble.

We can't have a sandcastle without a boy and a girl to build it. Let's try the boy first.

A circle for his head

two eyes

a smile

and some hair.

Put the hair, the eyes and the smile into the circle and you have the little boy's head.

Now practise some more heads – see what happens when you put the eyes higher up or wider apart – or make the smile not a smile.

Now he must have a body

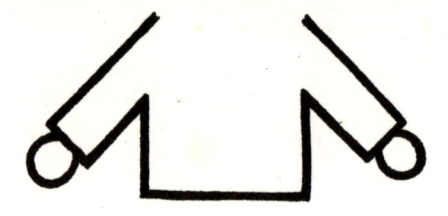

and pants

and legs

and feet.

Join them all on to the head. Colour him in with scribble or paint.

I like your little boy. He makes very good sandcastles, but a girl helped him.

Little girls usually have long hair, like this

otherwise you can draw her like the boy . . .

. . . a circle, two eyes, a smile and some long hair.

She can have a body like the boy

but little girls often wear skirts

and they have legs and feet like boys.

Now we have the girl and the boy who built the sandcastle. Let us call them

Susie

and

Dickon

Whilst playing at the seaside, Susie and Dickon found some rocks – (all straight lines!)

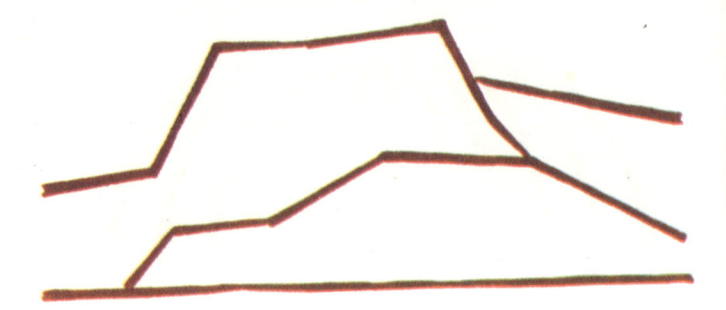

They had fun jumping off the rocks onto the sand –

just move their arms and legs about to make them jump.

Suddenly Susie saw a starfish, 'I can draw that in the sand!' she cried excitedly . . .

. . . and she drew it with simple curves joined together. Then she drew some smaller ones.

It doesn't matter if some of them aren't quite the right shape – they might be moving!

Some birds were flying overhead. 'They're easy' said Dickon, 'you only need two curves like these

and a few more curves to make the other birds. Then some big ones near us, and smaller ones as they get further away.'

The sun had been shining all this time. He's not difficult to draw. All you need is a circle and some lines . . .

He doesn't like shining on his own – he wants to be shining on the sea.

and you can fill him in with scribble or, if you are using paints, with solid colour.

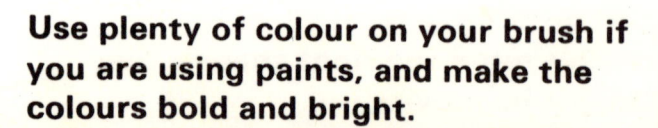

Use plenty of colour on your brush if you are using paints, and make the colours bold and bright.

The sea likes to have a boat sailing on it, and some birds flying overhead. Then yellow scribble for the sand.

Dickon and Susie want to wave to the boat as it sails past.

And they are going to play with the sandcastle, and jump on the rocks, which you colour in with scribble.

The boat is sailing away so it is getting smaller. Oh yes, we almost forgot the starfish. There that is everything. Now you can draw the seaside can't you!

Dickon and Susie have been very busy at the seaside. They are both feeling thirsty. 'There's an ice cream van' shouts Dickon, 'let's have an ice cream'

This is part of the body of the ice cream van

and this is the rest of the body. They fit together like this.

Now add two wheels, the driver and the window

and put some colours on the body. See how the colours change when you overlap them.

Try drawing some other cars and lorries.

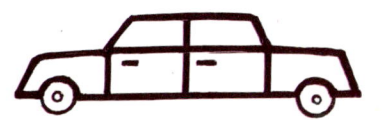

To get their ice creams, Dickon and Susie have to ask their mummy and daddy for some money. They find them sitting on the beach in deck chairs under an umbrella. Let's draw the umbrella first because it is so easy. Again each new line or lines in colour.

You see!

Now mummy . . .

Finish her in colour.

. . . and daddy

Mummy and daddy together under the umbrella waiting to be asked for an ice cream.

See how you move the position of Dickon's and Susie's eyes to make them look at their mummy and daddy.

'You know' said Dickon, after they had almost eaten their ice cream, 'ice cream cornets are like sea shells — let's see if we can find lots of different shells.'

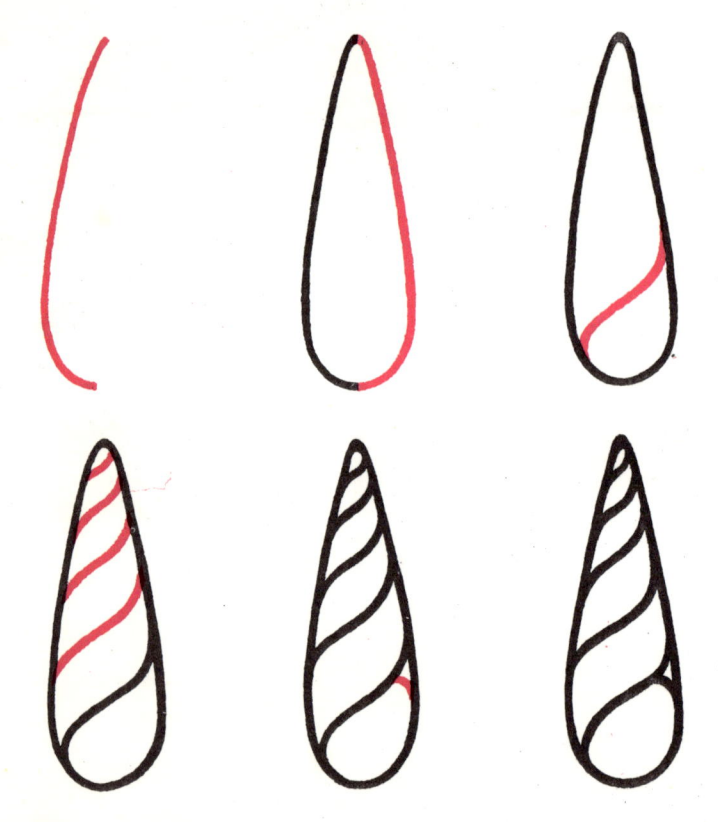

This is a pretty one — just made up from lines and circles

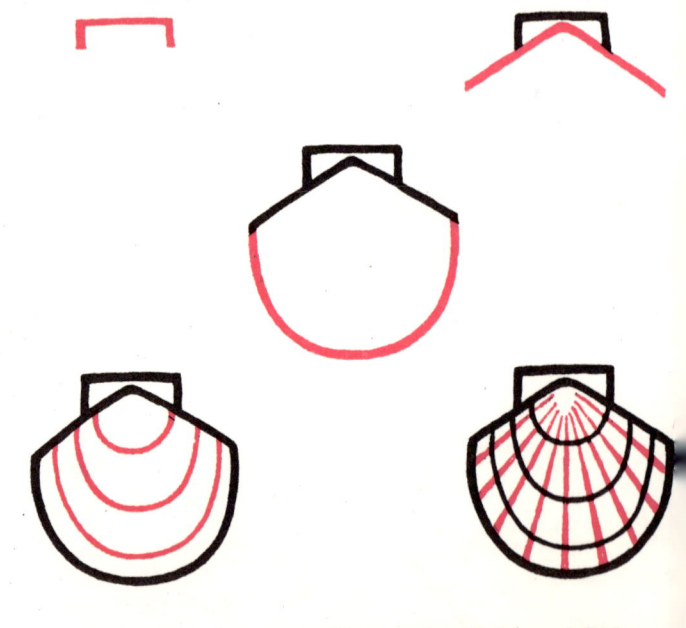

This one is like an ice cream cornet up-side-down.

and this is a scallop-shell in which oysters are sometimes served.

While they were looking for sea shells, Dickon and Susie found a crab. They never thought they would be able to draw him, but their daddy showed them an easy way. 'It is made up mainly of curved lines,' he told them.

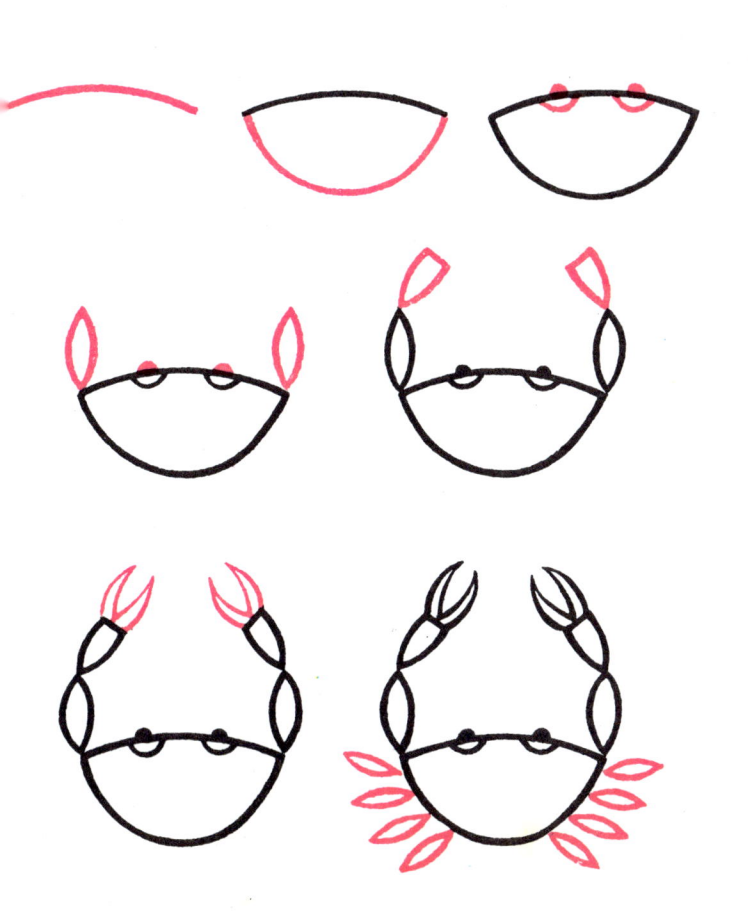

'I would like to draw a lighthouse like that one over there', said Susie 'and we could draw it at night time with its light shining.' 'Let's get the shape right first of all — we only need straight and curved lines,' her daddy told her.

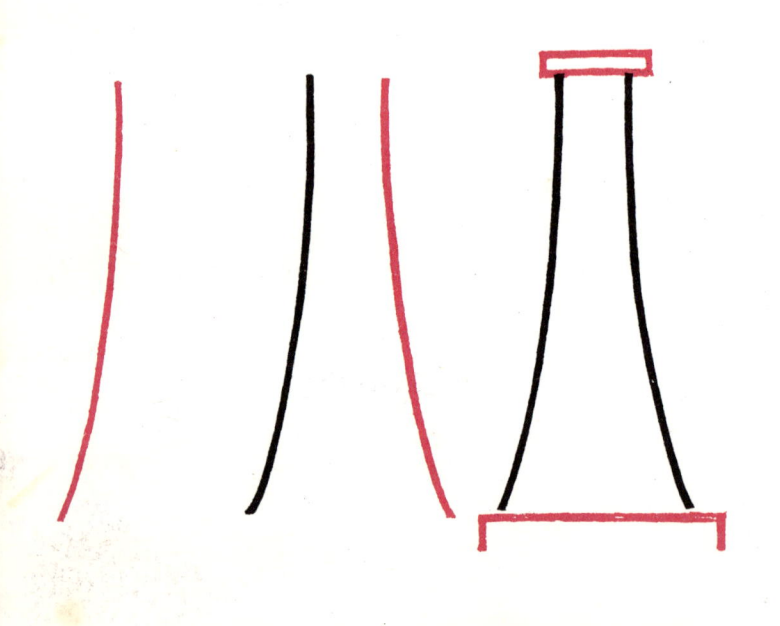

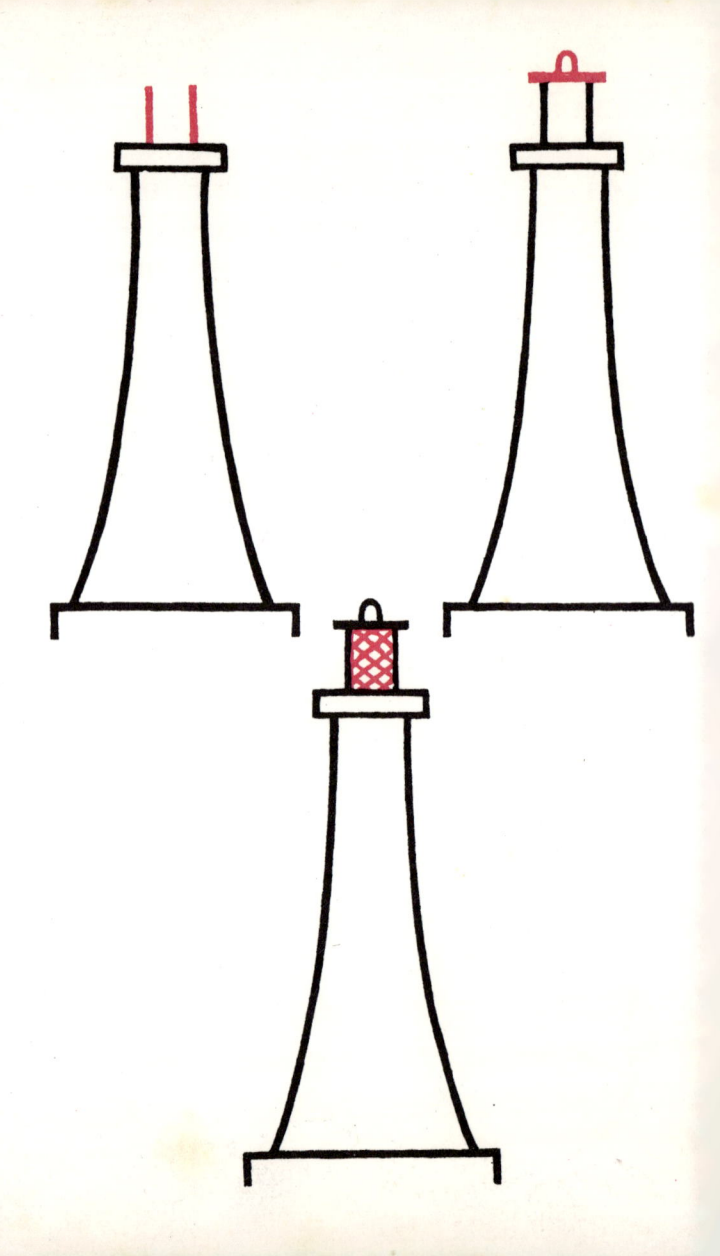

'Now we have drawn the outline of the lighthouse, we can add the sea and sky. Use scribble for the sky, or thick paint, and black scribble or paint between the waves. Leave the paper white to make the light shining from the lighthouse.'

'That is beautiful' cried Dickon and Susie excitedly, 'but is there anything else which warns the ships of danger?' 'Yes' replied their daddy, 'lightships can be anchored near sandbanks where it is impossible to build lighthouses. Let's draw one.'

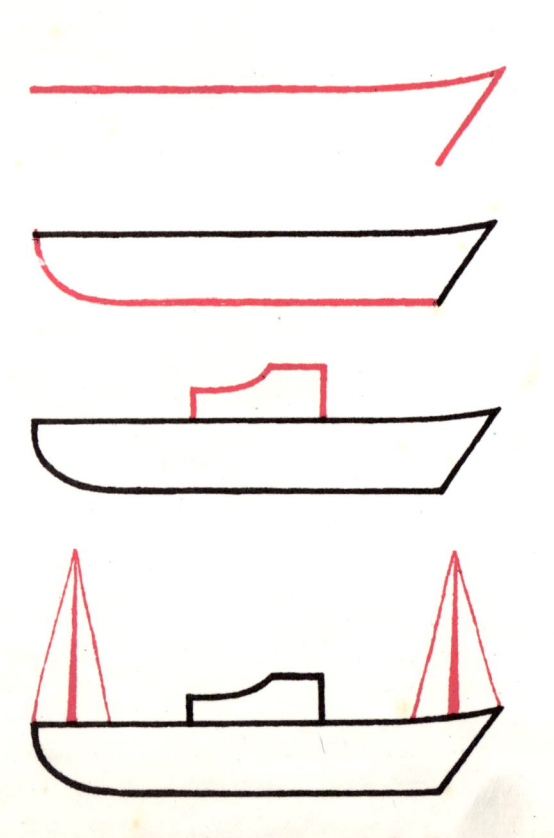

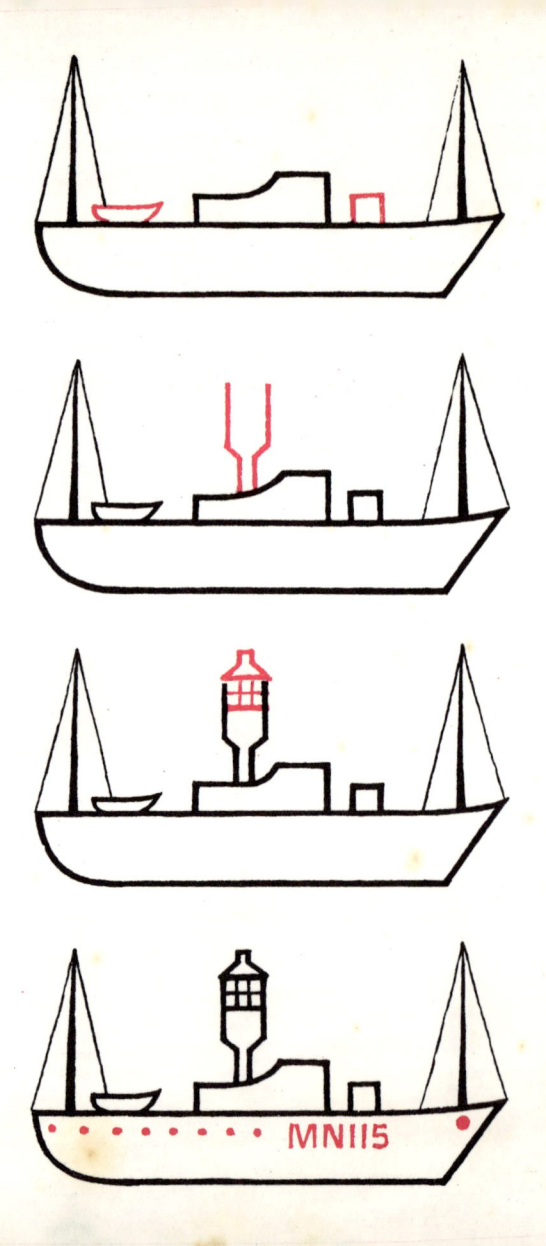

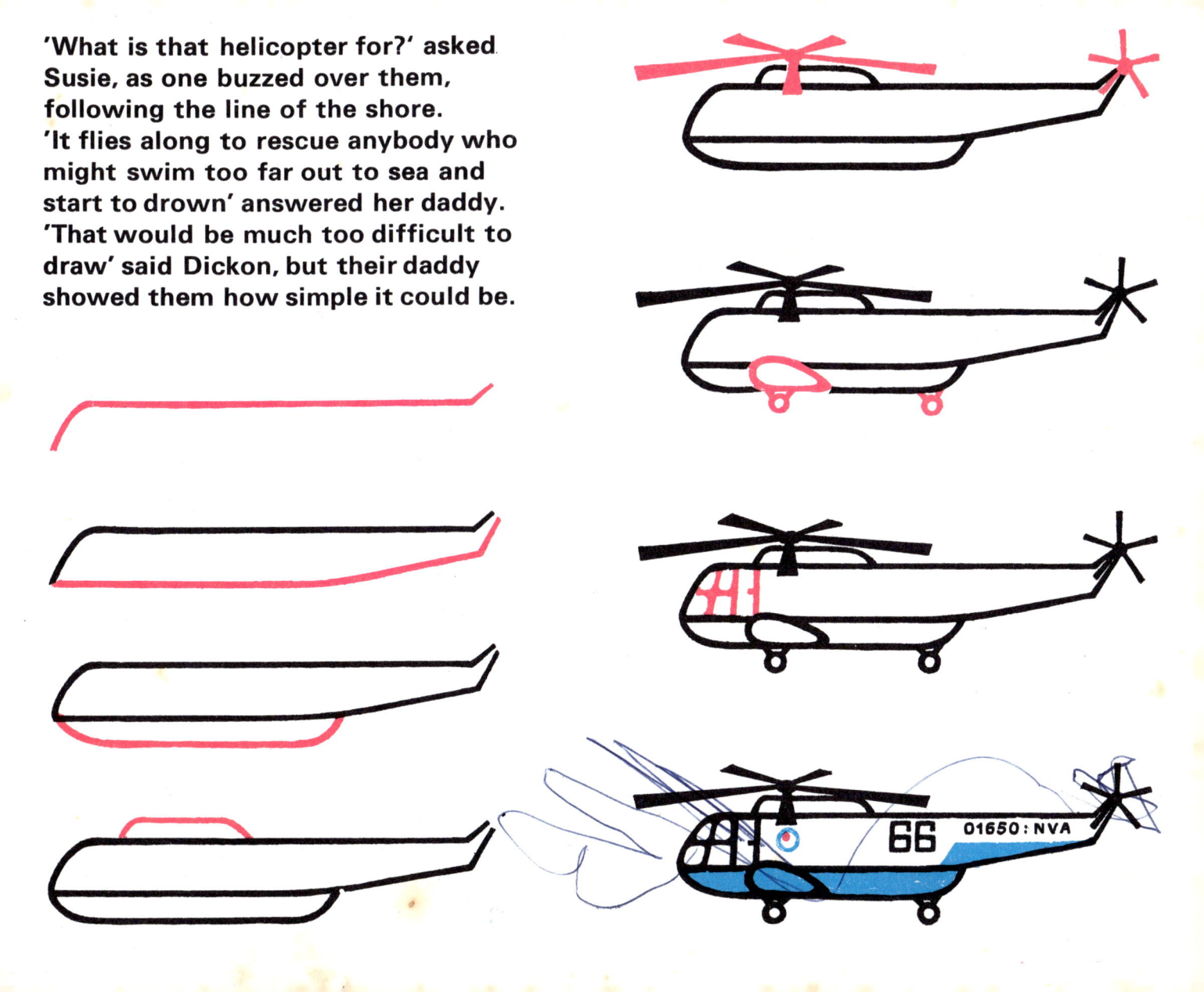

'What is that helicopter for?' asked Susie, as one buzzed over them, following the line of the shore. 'It flies along to rescue anybody who might swim too far out to sea and start to drown' answered her daddy. 'That would be much too difficult to draw' said Dickon, but their daddy showed them how simple it could be.

'After all that excitement, I think a quiet game of cricket on the beach would be a good idea' said daddy. Dickon and Susie agreed happily – 'Mummy must play as well' cried Susie. Mummy regretfully left her comfortable deck chair to join then. See how you move daddy's arms to make him hold the bat.

After a while Mummy, who didn't think cricket was such a quiet game after all, said she thought it was time for tea. 'Come and sit down children while daddy helps me with the picnic basket and all the food.'

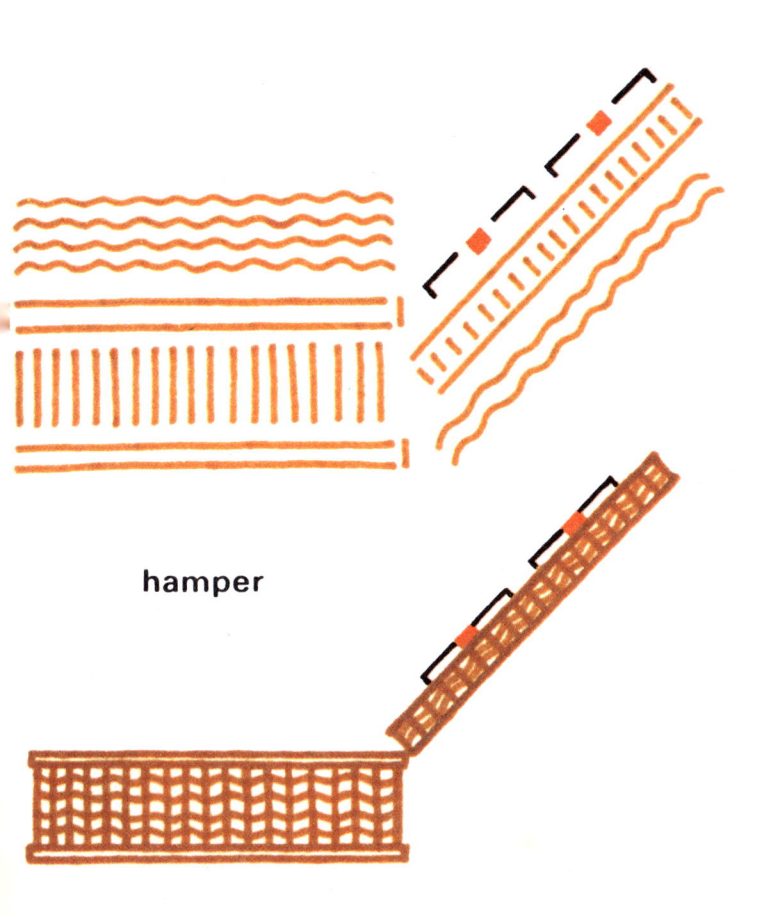

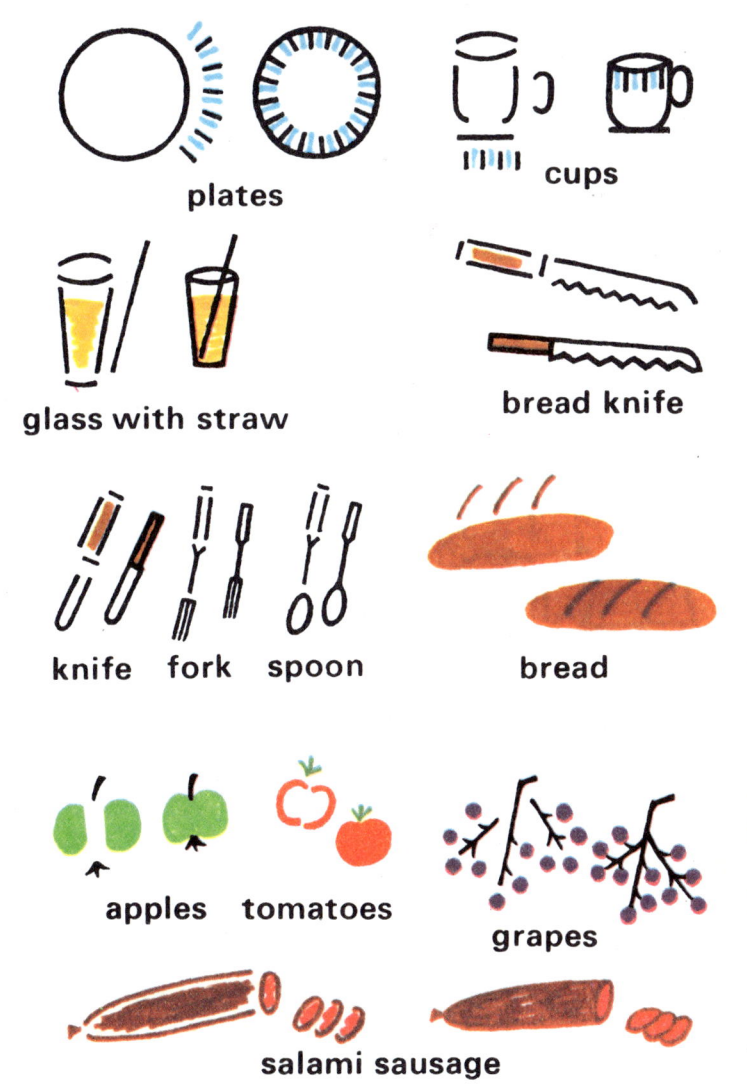

plates

cups

glass with straw

bread knife

knife fork spoon

bread

hamper

apples tomatoes grapes

salami sausage

Can you think of any more things which might be in the basket?

'We'll make some more big pictures after tea,' said their daddy. Dickon and Susie jumped for joy. This is just what they were longing to do.

Dickon and Susie jumping for joy!

'Let us start,' continued daddy, 'by drawing a view of the beach and the sea, with the people on it very small. This is how you would see it if you were standing on a cliff some distance away.'

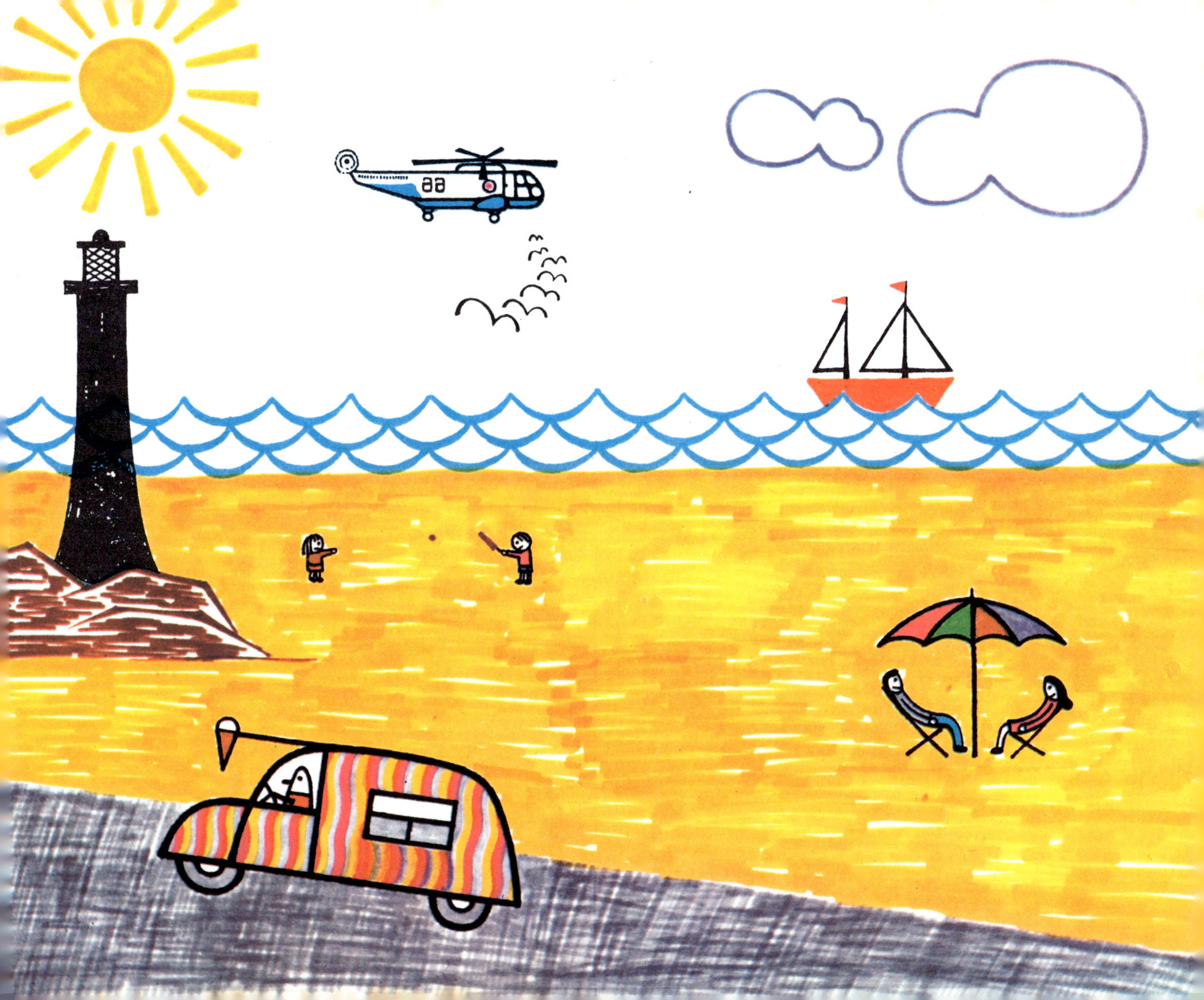

'To finish off' said daddy, 'we will do one last picture showing the crabs and the fishes swimming about in the sea. We can have a lot of fun with this, and make up some odd fishes of our own. I will start and you two can carry on.'

This is what he drew.

And this is what Dickon and Susie drew . . . now off you go and draw your own special pictures — and have lots of fun.